Finding Christ in the Crisis

FINDING CHRIST
in the
CRISIS

What the Pandemic Can Teach Us

By Father Harrison Ayre
and Michael R. Heinlein

Our Sunday Visitor
Huntington, Indiana

Nihil Obstat
Msgr. Michael Heintz, Ph.D.
Censor Librorum

Imprimatur
✠ Kevin C. Rhoades
Bishop of Fort Wayne-South Bend
September 28, 2020

Except where noted, the Scripture citations used in this work are taken from the *New American Bible, revised edition* © 2010, 1991, 1986, 1970 Confraternity of Christian Doctrine, Washington, D.C., and are used by permission of the copyright owner. All rights reserved. No part of the *New American Bible* may be reproduced in any form without permission in writing from the copyright owner.

Every reasonable effort has been made to determine copyright holders of excerpted materials and to secure permissions as needed. If any copyrighted materials have been inadvertently used in this work without proper credit being given in one form or another, please notify Our Sunday Visitor in writing so that future printings of this work may be corrected accordingly.

Our Sunday Visitor Publishing Division
Our Sunday Visitor Inc.
200 Noll Plaza
Huntington, IN 46750
www.osv.com
1-800-348-2440

ISBN: 978-1-68192-773-2 (Inventory No. T2645)
1. RELIGION—Christian Living—Devotional.
2. RELIGION—Christian Living—Spiritual Growth.
3. RELIGION—Christianity—Catholic.

eISBN: 978-1-68192-774-9
LCCN: 2020947054

Cover design: Tyler Ottinger
Cover art: Adobe Stock
Interior design: Amanda Falk
Interior art: Public Domain Images

PRINTED IN THE UNITED STATES OF AMERICA

For Fr. Anthony Sciarappa, my podcasting cohost, who helped me form much of what we wrote about, and with whom I sincerely enjoy recording every week.

— Fr. Harrison Ayre

For my grandparents, John and Betty, whose lives changed drastically during the pandemic, even as they celebrated their sixtieth wedding anniversary. In gratitude for their witness of faith and love.

— Michael R. Heinlein

Contents

Contents

Introduction

The COVID-19 pandemic has been hard on all of us. As Catholics, we suffered real loss with the closure of churches in the spring of 2020 and the ongoing restrictions on celebration of the sacraments. As time has worn on, the spiritual desert we have collectively experienced and the challenge of finding new ways to keep the Lord's Day have been difficult and painful. We struggle to make sense of the global crisis, and even of decisions made by Church leaders to protect our health and well-being. People's reactions to church closures and reopenings have covered a whole spectrum, from gratitude to anger and frustration.

The Church is always called to read the "signs of the times" in light of our faith. So, in the midst of everything we face with this pandemic, we need to ask: Is God speaking right now? How do we hear and see God in this moment? How do we listen for his voice?

If we want to hear the voice of God and see his actions in the world, we need to be a people who love the truth, because Jesus is the Truth. Truth, though, is not something we determine; rather, it is something revealed, something to which we submit. In this time of global uncertainty, there has been a steady rise in unhealthy distrust of legitimate authorities and professionals. Whether by self-appointed "experts" who skew the facts to their advantage, or those who use things such as a pandemic for political gain, truth has become relativized. As Cardinal Francis E. George, O.M.I., once observed, "For too many, politics is the ultimate horizon of their thinking and acting."

In order to hear God in this moment, we must seek him as the Truth and approach the facts surrounding the pandemic with humility. Only then can we hear the Truth speak to us *through* the reality of suffering, even during this worldwide pandemic.

If we want to arrive at truth, we have to acknowledge that truth is objective — and that we are not the arbiters of truth. Now more than ever, we need to reclaim the Catholic way of arriving at truth. Discovering the truth is not based on our own judgment of the facts, but on the acceptance of a Person who speaks to us the truth about man, life, the world, and God. To borrow a line from the Nicene Creed, Truth himself reveals to us "all things visible and invisible." This is especially important in our current context, where our sense of what is true is becoming increasingly distorted.

And truth goes hand in hand with charity, which has been largely missing from the conversations surrounding the response to the pandemic. Yet, charity must be our guiding principle as Catholics — and the way we handle the pandemic is no exception. Christian charity means willing the good of the other and working toward it. Desiring the common good and striving toward it is a requirement of charity, as Pope Benedict XVI wrote in his encyclical *Caritas in Veritate*. In addition, he said, "When animated by charity, commitment to the common good has greater worth than a merely secular and political stand would have" (7). In society, there are many ways of discerning what the common good might be. But charity provides needed clarity, particularly directed toward the poor and vulnerable. Charity and truth, together, form the way forward.

As we consider truth in this situation, we need to be aware of three problematic attitudes surrounding the pandemic that have further distorted our perception of truth. These attitudes have shown themselves often in these past months, and all are ultimately contrary to the Faith. The attitudes are denial, fear, and neo-gnosticism.

Some deny the pandemic altogether, saying it is a hoax. This is not based on a

Catholic understanding of truth, but a relativistic one, guided primarily by ideology. Those who see this pandemic as a hoax have set themselves up as public health and statistical experts, though most have no experience in either field. Others see the pandemic as a conspiracy, a secret attempt by those in power to overthrow or further control society. The Catholic vision of truth depends on the reasonableness of things, relying on data and evidence to support such claims — something conspiracies and hoaxes are unable to offer.

The second response, fear, is certainly reasonable to an extent. Especially in the early days of the pandemic, as we saw death tolls rising, as government policies changed our daily lives, and as misinformation made its way around social media, fear and anxiety were a normal human response. But there were extreme expressions of fear as well. For example, many of the faithful expressed fears that church closures and limited access to the sacraments would keep us from receiving sufficient grace to aid us in this time. It seems, unfortunately, many of us have forgotten the perpetual grace we have in our baptism.

The final problematic response we want to address can be identified as neo-gnosticism. The heresy of gnosticism arose in the early Church, but it has continued in the life of the Church in varying forms to this day. Gnostics see the body as not only unimportant but as in competition with the spirit, and they believe that the body ought to give way to the only true good: the spiritual. Time and again over the course of the pandemic, different figures in the Church — laity and clergy alike — have expressed serious concerns about all things spiritual, often at the expense of our humanity. To speak of the spiritual is obviously not a bad thing, but it should never be at the cost or neglect of our full humanity. Our physical well-being is not in competition with our spiritual well-being; on the contrary, we have a duty to take care of both.

Catholic tradition gives great dignity to the full human person, which includes the physical aspect and not just the spiritual. Pope Benedict XVI aptly describes this: "Precisely because in man there is more than mere *bios* (living matter), biological life too becomes infinitely precious. It is not possible to dispose of man because he is endowed with the dignity of God." Because we are made in God's image, even the body has a dignity and a preciousness that is worthy of protecting. When we look after our own health and that of others, we respect the image of God in each human being.

The neo-gnostic attitude also ignores the holistic way in which Jesus went about his ministry: He forgave sins *and* healed. While it is true our embodiedness is of a lesser importance — "And do not be afraid of those who kill the body but cannot kill the soul; rather, be afraid of the one who can destroy both soul and body in Gehenna" (Mt 10:28) — that does not endorse the dismissal of our duty and obligation to care for the health and well-being of our brothers and sisters. Neo-gnosticism, at its heart, rejects our embodiedness and sees the spiritual as the only truly real thing — a direct contradiction not only of the creation account in Genesis, but a denial of the central importance of the Incarnation as well.

We need to be able to read the signs of the times with docility. What's missing in discourse right now is a true spiritual interpretation of this moment, rooted in charity. As we have witnessed, especially in the early days of the pandemic, the closure of a parish church may be necessary in pursuit of general public health and safety, but what is God saying and doing when this happens?

Right now, a lot of us feel abandoned not only by the Church, but even by God. We lack a spiritual interpretation of this moment and are unable to discern God's presence at this time. The goal of this book is to begin to shed light on what God might be saying to us now, both in the Church and in the world. Using scriptural interpretation and examining particular realities of faith, we aim to identify what God expects of us and what he is trying to say to us in this challenging time. The path forward through the pandemic is, as in every circumstance of life for Christians, to follow Jesus Christ, who is the way, the truth, and the life. And his way is the way of the Cross — the way of charity and self-sacrifice for others.

While we may at times be restricted in our access to the Eucharist, and even to pastoral leadership, the effects of this pandemic are by no means a defeat. Instead, as men and women of faith, we should find in this time an opportunity to rediscover the heart of our Catholic identity as a baptized people. We will reflect also on the life and ministry of Saint Damien of Molokai, who provides a lived example of the importance of addressing physical and spiritual needs as a cohesive whole, even in the face of deadly illness. In his life and legacy, the whole Church can better understand the fruits of what this moment can offer.

I.

The Faith and the Pandemic

LEARNING FROM ISRAEL

How do we discern God's action in history? What tools does he give us? Too often we attempt to grasp at this understanding in an individualistic way. In the seclusion of our own prayers and thoughts, we ask, "God, how am I to make sense of what's happening right now?" This is not wrong in and of itself, but we can forget, or perhaps do not know, the tools that help us see things more from God's perspective and less from our own narrow perspective. One of the lenses through which Catholics discern God's work in the world is that of Scripture. For us, Scripture is not just a historical document, but the living word of God that brings the past, present, and future together. The events and stories of biblical history help us understand and see how God is still at work among us.

As Catholics, we believe the "New Testament lies hidden in the Old and the Old Testament is unveiled in the New" (*Catechism of the Catholic Church* 129). This gives the Old Testament a constant relevance, because at its heart, it points the way to Christ. Since the Church is Christ's body, as Saint Paul often teaches in his letters, we see the Church prefigured in the Old Testament as well. In fact, throughout her history, the Church has referred to the Old Testament to see how God was speaking to the Church, seeing in the lessons from the old covenant an interpretation of the current historical moment.

And so a reflection on the trials, tribulations, and sufferings of Israel in the Old Testament can be a stalwart guide for seeing God's hand active today in the Church, the New Israel. To illustrate this, consider the story of Israel's Babylonian captivity. Although grieved and suffering, Israel also saw in its own captivity a manifestation of God's power to rescue it from that suffering. This story offers a great deal of clarity for the Church to see God's hand in our own time.

Prophesied by Jeremiah, Nebuchadnezzar — the king of Babylon — was an agent of God (see Jer 25:9) who brought an end to Israel's possession of the land. The Babylonians gradually overtook Israel, sent a large portion of the Israelites out of Israel, destroyed the Temple in Jerusalem, and removed the power of the Davidic line of kings. These three things — the land, the Temple, and the king— were all at the heart of Israel's identity. With the Babylonian exile, everything about who the Israelites were had been removed.

The Psalmist captures the sadness of

the situation:

> By the rivers of Babylon
>> there we sat weeping
>> when we remembered Zion.
> On the poplars in its midst
>> we hung up our harps.
> For there our captors asked us
>> for the words of a song;
> Our tormentors, for joy:
>> "Sing for us a song of Zion!"
> But how could we sing a song of
>> the LORD
>> in a foreign land? (Psalm 137:1–
>> 4)

Israel's reaction to the exile was rightly one of sadness, abandonment, and desolation. Suddenly, everything they thought made them a people favored by God was gone. What the Israelites discovered in their exile was that even when their identity was so deeply shaken, it could be found in their memory. Thus the Psalmist urged God's people to remember Jerusalem as their highest joy.

But Israel did not remain in exile forever. King Cyrus of Persia gave the Israelites permission to return to their land after he conquered Babylon. Ezra-Nehemiah recounts Israel's joyful return. In rebuilding the city, the exiles were suddenly freed. They saw the hand of God leading them back to what he promised. The Temple was rebuilt, and sacrifice was offered again. Especially under Ezra's leadership, a religious revival instilled a new fervor in observing God's commandments. In all this, Israel saw God's action; they saw God's universal power. Their God was not just the God of Israel among other gods, whose reign was limited to one place, but he also was able to work beyond the boundaries of the promised land to bring Israel back to its inheritance.

While there is much more to the story, this brief survey gives us a sense of how the Church, as the new Israel, can learn from Israel's exile. While COVID-19 imposes limitations on our worship, we can reflect on how God is acting in the Church today and find meaning for our present moment.

Israel's sadness and destitution were real, and the same is true for the Church right now. We have seen limited access to the sacraments, reduced numbers at Mass, and limitations on ministry. It seems that the normal ways we live our faith have been suddenly and violently taken away from us. These losses are real and are deeply felt, not only by each Catholic individually, but even more deeply in the heart of the Church. Suddenly, the very things that comprise the heart of our Christian identity were taken away from us. The psalmist's lament in Psalm 137 really is the lament of the Church in these difficult times: How can we sing songs of joy?

This sadness and dejection leads to uncovering a second interpretive key from Israel's story for the Church: purification. God used Israel's exile to draw his people back to their covenant, to get back to their mission of being a light to the nations. God had to remove a lot from Israel in order for them to see their mission clearly again.

In a similar way, what we now face offers the opportunity for deep purification of the Church. While we lament the loss of the sacramental life, perhaps God is taking away the things that give us life and identity as a means to call us to conversion. This is not to say, of course, that God directly brought about the virus. Rather, God can and will use this historical event — as he has done time and again throughout history — to purify the Church and bring us closer to his heart.

As God purified Israel while in exile and moved his people to recall the covenant he had established, so too he is purifying the Church today, calling us to repentance and to a return to the heart of the Christian life. The scandals of the clergy, the lukewarmness of faith, and so much more call us to repent. Might God be drawing us into a time of purification to recommit ourselves to the covenant and mission he has established in his Church?

Despite the sadness and dejection Israel faced, they carried hope in their hearts, as seen in Psalm 137. Even as they lamented the loss of Jerusalem, their homeland, and the promises of God that came with the land, Israel refused to forget, and therein they found their hope. Despite the horror and sadness of the exile, their refusal to forget Jerusalem was the refusal to let go of their identity. In doing so, they showed that they trusted that God would somehow turn their memory into reality once more in the future. In their suffering, they yearned for God to act even in Babylon and to draw them back home.

The people of Israel learned anew that God is the primary actor in history, not them. By this lesson, they rediscovered God and began to turn to him again in the land of their exile, far from the place where they had once encountered him. Here they found the hope that sustained them in their suffering. The memory of God's actions in the past helped them see God as active in their present. Though they were lost, and everything that defined them was taken away, they examined themselves, looked to God's actions in the past, and came to know that God had never abandoned them. Having repented of their sin, they remembered that God was a merciful Father who heard their prayers. God gave Israel a space to work through their emotions and their spiritual state in order to come back to him with all their hearts.

This is a message of hope for the Church today. So much seems to have been stolen from us by the pandemic and its effects, but God is still with us. We still have his promise that the gates of hell will never prevail against our Church (see Mt 16:18) and that he will remain with us always.

Like Israel, how can we begin to see this moment as an opportunity to grow in our relationship with God, for whom "all things are possible" (Mt 19:26)? As Saint Paul taught, "We know that all things work for good for those who love God" (Rom 8:28). We should begin asking:

- What can the temporary loss of sacraments do to reinvigorate our relationship with God and the Church?

- What must we do to reevaluate our relationship with Christ, his Church, and his sacraments?
- Are we truly living the mission for which he has commissioned us?

God uses our history to bring us closer to himself. Understanding this is essential to seeing God's action in the present. As God used the Babylonian exile for Israel's good, he can use this pandemic to draw his Church closer to himself through Christ. God's freedom never overwhelms, but always cooperates with humanity. That can help us understand the events of our world without falling into discouragement or despair.

SOME THEOLOGICAL LESSONS

With the suspension of public Masses and the disruption of ecclesial life during this time of pandemic, many Catholics feel disconnected from Christ and the Church. Certainly, the inability to receive the Eucharist during weeks of canceled Masses in the spring of 2020 was felt acutely. But despite the challenges, this time also has been one of opportunity — one in which God calls us more fully to appreciate the gifts he gives us, particularly related to the sacraments and ecclesial life.

Many Catholics were understandably stunned and shaken by the temporary loss of public worship. Some even felt unable to support the decisions that were made by our bishops. Yet as Catholics, we can be assured that the Church was right to proceed with caution amid the coronavirus pandemic. Given how little we knew about the virus early on in the outbreak, it was both prudent and consistent with protecting the common good, which is always a principal aim in the Church's decision-making process.

While it might not have been an easy experience for the faithful, the caution displayed by the institutional Church did not equate to an abandonment of what is most central to the Catholic Faith, which is rooted in baptism, the Eucharist, and ministry. As baptized Christians, we already are equipped with many spiritual goods that provide for us the means to survive such a challenge.

Baptism

The reality is that, even when we are separated from the sacraments — even the Eucharist — we are never alone, and we are never abandoned. This is because we have been baptized in Christ. Rather than a one-time historical event, baptism is a way of being, and through the waters of baptism we began a new life and a new mode of existence. Thanks to our baptism, we are truly alive in Christ. Or, as Saint Paul acknowledges, Christ lives in us (see Gal 2:20).

Christ tells us that he is the vine, and we are the branches (see Jn 15:5). When we are baptized, he makes us members of his own body, and we are thus forever changed and made one with him. Why is this especially significant during times of distress and separation from the Eucharistic assembly? Because by nature of our baptism, wherever we are, Christ, too, is present. And that bond to Christ never goes away.

Our baptism is a portal through which we are able to continue seeking and achieving deeper levels of communion with Christ, even if churches are locked or Masses are unavailable. Christians throughout the ages have relied on this reality of singular importance, and especially in times of tragedy and chaos this truth of our baptism should be a great source of consolation.

Through our baptism, Christ is present to us in different ways and with varying intensities. This is similar to any relationship, in which the people we love can be present to us in the flesh, through social media, on the telephone, in a letter or photograph, or through memories. Our faith teaches us that, because we are one with Christ in baptism, he is always with us. He is present in the Scriptures, which the Second Vatican

Council called "food of the soul" (*Dei Verbum*, 21). And, of course, Christ is present body, blood, soul, and divinity in the Eucharist, his greatest gift to us. During times when we cannot receive him or be with him in the Eucharist, however, our bond with Christ through baptism makes spiritual communion possible, too — a practice made especially popular by the pandemic.

As baptized Christians, we gain life in Christ and are able to live and love like him. Or, according to the line Saint Paul borrowed: "In him we live and move and have our being" (Acts 17:28). Living with and for Christ means we are able to worship the Father in imitation of and union with the Son, always and everywhere. In fact, Saint Paul exhorts us in Romans 12:1 to live our lives as one continuous act of worship, giving glory to God in all of our thoughts, words, and deeds. Because of this, the idea of sacrifice is connected to worship in a very real way. Just as Christ laid himself down in love of the Father and for our good, so are we called to do the same.

This time of pandemic offers us the opportunity to better understand, contemplate, and more fully embrace what it means to be a baptized Christian. Through a deeper understanding of our baptism, we can make our homes into domestic churches and bring Christ to the world around us, so that our lives become acts of worship as we take on the call to holiness with greater resolve.

Eucharist

The Sacraments of Baptism and the Eucharist are closely intertwined. It is baptism that makes it possible for us to receive the Eucharist. But baptism also enables us to live the Eucharist. In baptism we have "put on Christ" (see Gal 3:27). That means that with him we, too, are called to offer our very lives in sacrifice, to share in his cross. By the power of the Eucharist, our crosses are joined to Christ's own, and we are given the strength we need to persevere.

In the celebration of the Eucharist, a priest gathers up all of our prayers, praises, and sacrifices and, standing in our place and in the place of Christ as head of his body, makes present Christ's sacrifice of praise on Calvary. In that same action, our sacrifice is joined to his. This reality should bring us great comfort even in the midst of a pandemic, when we might not be able to make it to Mass. Because of our unity in Christ's body through baptism, even when we are not physically present at the Eucharistic sacrifice, each of us is united to every Mass. Because of this, the Eucharist is the source and summit of the Christian life. Our own involvement in this is essential to allowing the graces from this to take root in our own lives. We must be intentional about it, therefore, perhaps calling this reality to mind when we make an act of spiritual communion, or by utilizing technological means such as viewing a live stream of the Mass.

It can also be reassuring to remember that the Eucharist is not the only means by which Christ imparts his grace. The pandemic has been an occasion to remember

— and to live out in a very real way — that God's action is not bound to the sacraments. Yes, Christ established the sacraments as the ordinary means by which we have access to the divine life. But because we are members of Christ's body, God's grace is not kept at a distance when, through no fault of our own, we are unable to partake in the sacraments. In such extraordinary circumstances, God's grace should not be understood as distant or inaccessible. God is all-loving and all-powerful and will never abandon us. Rather, God provides for those who turn to him in total confidence and love. And there is no expiration date to the graces he makes available to us in the sacraments we have received in the past.

While the sacraments are chief among Christ's gifts to us, we also remember that this gift is received on the terms of the giver, who is Christ. In turn, Christ gives his gifts to us through the hierarchy of the Church (our bishops and their collaborators, the priests), who stand in his place. And so the gifts bestowed by Christ in the sacraments ought never be demanded by the faithful, but instead received in gratitude. When Church leaders decided to suspend public celebration of the sacraments during the early days of the pandemic in 2020 — and if they should decide to do so again as they deem appropriate — they have the authority to do so. Our best response is rooted in an attempt to understand, in obedience and love.

In times of crisis, it is only natural to look for ways to make things normal again. When we are trying to do so, it is important to be sure we are thinking with the Church and not presenting, although well-intentioned, inaccurate material about the Faith. While the Eucharist is the source and summit of our faith, we need to be careful about how we express that. If we are unable to receive the Eucharist (or other sacraments) through no fault of our own, such as amid a pandemic, we are not cut off from God's grace. God is not abandoning us when we cannot receive the Eucharist in such circumstances. Although it is the ordinary means to access the divine life, receiving the sacraments alone does not have a real effect in our lives. Our own cooperation with God's grace is needed for them to be effective, and so the sacraments are not spiritual personal protective equipment. Grace is not a magic remedy for humanity's fallenness, but rather a lifeline God gives us to cooperate with him and enter into his life.

As gifts of Christ, the sacraments are to be received in love. Gifts are not to be demanded or seen as rights. The Church's law at times uses language that refers to the rights the faithful have regarding the sacraments, but these laws exist to ensure the gifts are made available to the faithful on Christ's terms and not on ours. It is clear even in the law that the sacraments are mediated by the hierarchy, and any decisions made to impose a temporary suspension on the celebration must be rooted in charity.

This can be a challenge if we slide into thinking of sacraments purely on an individual basis. But the sacraments are a communion with the entire Church, because communion with Christ is communion with all who constitute his body. In the end, reception of the sacraments is meant for the good of the Church and humanity, which is to say more than just for our own good. Reception of the sacraments is meant to be fruitful and lead us "to practice charity" (see *Sacrosanctum Concilium,* 59). And Vatican II reiterates that, even if we are members of Christ's body and receive the sacraments, etc., we are not saved if we do not "persevere in charity" (*Lumen Gentium,* 14).

Even when public Masses were suspended due to the pandemic, our bishops and priests continued to celebrate the Eucharist, and many of them livestreamed those Masses. Such means, then, could be seen as the twenty-first-century way of allowing the faithful to facilitate the reality of their union with the Church's worship — not unlike Saint Charles Borromeo's request for priests to celebrate outdoor Masses so the faithful could watch from their homes during epidemics in the sixteenth century.

While attending Mass in person is

the ordinary means of participation (because we live an incarnated faith), we have a unique opportunity for spiritual growth when we cannot attend physically. Can we imagine how we might still be able to live the Faith despite the temporary inability to attend Mass or receive Christ in the Eucharist? Even a time of challenge can be an opportunity to clarify and deepen our understanding of the sacrament.

One of the many ancient titles given to the Eucharist is the "sacrament of charity." The celebration of the Eucharist makes charity itself present because it makes Christ himself present. Christ tells us, "No one has greater love than this, to lay down one's life for one's friends" (Jn 15:13). While he modeled this through his cross, he also gave us the model of love and service to others as our everyday means to share his witness. We see this especially in his washing of the feet of his disciples. When we follow his model of service, we are living Eucharistically. As Pope Benedict XVI wrote in his encyclical *Deus Caritas Est*, "A Eucharist which does not pass over into the concrete practice of love is intrinsically fragmented."

Sadly, the Eucharist became a point of contention for many Catholics in the midst of the pandemic. Among other things, the encouragement to receive Communion in the hand and the requirement to wear a face mask when inside a church have entailed a sacrifice of significant personal piety on our part. Yet we can find comfort in the knowledge that the sacraments are Christ's gifts, mediated by the hierarchy. Receiving Communion in the hand is not a violation of revelation or ecclesial tradition. And while wearing a face mask might be uncomfortable or an annoyance, we can recognize, through charity, that it is a reasonable request for the good of others. We are rarely asked to forfeit personal preferences or comfort. This time of pandemic has proven to be an exception. But when we respond in obedience, giving of ourselves for others, we find true liberty.

Finally, this moment can remind us that there is enough grace in the Eucharist

— even in one reception of Communion — to make us saints. In the Eucharist Jesus gives his complete self to the Church, a gift that strengthens us, but remains and does not disappear. If it were to disappear, then we would be falling into magical thinking, where we need to receive the Eucharist as often as possible in order to be a saint. Rather, when we receive Communion, God's grace is given fully, because Christ gives himself fully to us. It is a healthy reminder that "frequent" reception of the Eucharist for many of the saints of the Church meant a few times a year. Among them are some of our greatest saints. And then there are the spiritual benefits of Eucharistic fasting spoken of by popes and saints. Times of absence from the Eucharist, such as during the pandemic, then, can help us to focus on how to act on the grace given in the past through the Eucharist. This can awaken within us a deeper hunger for the Bread of Life, which can allow its fruit to be manifested more intensely in our lives.

Ministry

There is no doubt that the pandemic will leave a mark on ecclesial life beyond the sacraments. The immediate shutting down of churches and schools, and the longer-term shift in operations, resulted in a financial loss that will never be recouped for many dioceses, parishes, and institutions. As a result, our Church is almost certain to have a much smaller institutional footprint in the future.

Within a few weeks of the pandemic coming to the United States, parishes and schools began reporting financial insolvency. Permanent closures were announced, and we continue to hear of more such closures. Dioceses, already suffering losses themselves, have not always been able to help parishes and schools stay afloat. The pandemic, in some ways, has rounded out a perfect storm for ecclesial institutions already suffering from shrinking revenue in the wake of the clergy sexual abuse crisis and an overall demographic decline in American church life. And then there is the real likelihood that some of the people who were unable or who chose not to come to Mass during the pandemic might never return in person. The pandemic undoubtedly will lead to a high degree of disengagement in ecclesial life, and those negative effects will outlast any threats to our physical health.

The pandemic, then, has further revealed both immediate and lasting problems for ecclesial life in the United States and Canada that demand a more effective response than a business-as-usual approach. The Church has long needed an honest reckoning regarding the decline in participation. Baptisms and marriages annually decrease in number. Clustering, merging, and closing parishes has become a norm in many North American dioceses. The once-sizable footprint of Catholic education and health care continues to dwindle.

But, as in the spiritual life, could the deleterious effects of the pandemic be an opportunity to reconsider our current approach to ministry? Do we need the massive institutional structures we now support? Is there a way our resources can be repurposed so that we can move away from maintaining an outdated structure, and get on with doing the work of the Gospel in ways that support the Church's mission more effectively? And how does a renewed and reinvigorated understanding of baptism play into this?

When the pandemic first hit, many Catholics rightfully identified a shortage in spiritual resources made available by dioceses or parishes that would help the faithful navigate these challenging times. As parish life was put on hold, some parishioners began accusing their pastors of not doing enough. Although several practical, extraordinary actions were taken, they were not enough to help the Church process this crisis. While there is no single magic bullet that will foster greater participation in the life of the Church, attempts must be made to reiterate what the faithful can and should be doing while separated from the community. In fact, a lasting result of the pandemic might be a renewed focus on the basics of Christian practice, which take place in our daily lives, rather than an overemphasis on activities in the parish. For the parish is not just the campus where Mass and activities happen, but it is the collection of all the faithful in a particular area. When we pray at home, that's an activity of the parish. When we hold a Bible study with some friends at a coffee shop, that's an activity of the parish, too.

Staying at home and being socially distant presents a new paradigm for the Church and an opportunity to re-envision a mission too often embodied by "doing" things. The Church exists to win souls for Christ. More than doing, this necessitates being. As we approach this new paradigm, we might consider what we have had to stop doing, and what the effects — positive or negative — have been. We also might take this time to reevaluate our programs, activities, and initiatives, prioritizing deeper prayer, a more penitential spirit, and a greater understanding of the importance of sacrifice. With such spiritual tools, it is clear that much of the practice of the Faith is already in the hands of the faithful. In this unique moment, when so much about ecclesial life is being stripped away from us, even if only for a time, we can allow God to transform and purify us. If used properly, this time of change and uncertainty can be leveraged as an opportunity to retool our approach to ministry for a more hopeful future.

As the pandemic and its effects continue, it may also be helpful to highlight the distinction between the duties of clergy and the laity. The clergy are at the service of the lay faithful, while the laity are charged with the sanctification of the world. While the clergy's ministry is internally oriented to the life of the Church, the laity's realm of service is directed to the entire society. It is clear, then, that any broad change to the Church's approach to ministry cannot be undertaken without the full enthusiasm and support of the laity. The clergy must do more to teach the laity about their role and duties, while continuing to fortify them with the sacraments and instruct them through preaching. This will only serve to facilitate the Church's mission, building up the lay apostolate that brings Christ to the world and the world to Christ.

Saint Paul speaks about the various ministries exercised by Christ's members. Each of us is called uniquely: "There are different kinds of spiritual gifts but the same Spirit; there are different forms of service but the same Lord; there are different workings but the same God who produces all of them in everyone" (1 Cor 12:4–6). It is through the ministries of the Church — performed by the members of Christ's body — that the world encounters Christ. As the late Cardinal George said, "The Church exists where the gifts of Christ are shared."

Properly "doing church" means coming to understand that parish life and parish activities are not ends in themselves. Rather, our activities and programs must be geared to facilitate the Church's mission of salvation. Such a vision must guide us if we are to do what Christ asks of us. It is not helpful to bind ourselves to various forms of ministry that are particular to the conditions of place and time. Every age brings forth new ways of carrying on Christ's work, and the forms of our ministries come and go, but the goals of our ministry remain the same. Our task, supported and sustained by God's grace and the guidance of the Holy Spirit, is to seize this moment and reflect upon what is necessary and what can fade away. In this way, we will be able to reallocate our resources to be more effective and, most importantly, find new ways to convert the world. Taking advantage of the opportunities presented by the coronavirus pandemic, we can welcome and allow to take root the new life God is always offering us.

II.
Holiness in the Pandemic

THE PATTERN OF THE CROSS

Earlier, we approached our reflection on the present moment through the lens of ancient Israel, and what that experience means for the Church. Now we will reflect on what significance the cross brings to this moment. Certainly, the two are not mutually exclusive. Israel's suffering foreshadows Christ's cross. And in that foreshadowing we can see how the cross's power has been active throughout history, even to the present time.

Everything that the people of Israel suffered was suffered by Jesus on the cross, for their own sake and for the life of the world. This is one of the reasons the Church can look so easily to Israel to help us understand the current moment: The whole history of Israel is summed up in Christ, which is, therefore, also true of the Church. The cross was already present in the time of Israel, and it is now always present in the Church and therefore connects the two testaments. In fact, the Church's natural state is the cross. It is the cross that redeems, and it is the cross that truly is the source of our hope.

Hope is the virtue whereby we really and truly recognize God's presence in all the events of life. Hope is the realization that God is here: He is here in the suffering, and he is here in the good. Because Christ enters our condition, especially entering into suffering and death, the cross is really the seat of hope. In the death of Jesus, we see a God who has gone to the limits of our condition to meet us there and to draw us up in his new life through his resurrection. Therefore, no suffering or difficulty is devoid of hope, because Christ has gone there before us, and he has given it meaning and made it holy.

As Saint Paul says, "For I resolved to know nothing while I was with you except Jesus Christ, and him crucified" (1 Cor 2:2). The cross, then — as the heart of Israel's life, the centrality of Christ's mission, and the heart of the Church — is the lens by which we read everything.

Because the cross is always active and effective, it is always drawing the Church into communion with Christ's saving mission. The difficulties of our present moment assuredly can be united to Christ's cross and saving mission. The cross is always a proposal to the Church, inviting us to embrace it as Christ's saving mission for the world, the source of our hope. And so we must constantly be reflecting: How do we live the hope of the cross through all this?

The cross, it must be remembered, is

not necessarily something we choose; often it is imposed from outside. Jesus' words to Saint Peter (that he would be led where he did not want to go — see John 21:18) re-iterate that the cross is not something we choose, but is given to us. When given, the cross offers us a choice: We can embrace it or run away from it. As Christians following Christ's way, we must go by the way of the cross if we want eternal life. By embracing the cross, by participating in Christ's saving mission, we are living the cross as a sign of hope: Hope is where God's grace works in us.

This reality is often lost on us in to-day's culture. Most of us have been raised with the therapeutic mindset that, should a wound or suffering arise, it must be healed almost instantly. This creates a Catholi-cism that focuses on comfort as a goal in itself and ignores the reality and depths of the cross. Yes, there are times when Christ heals and removes suffering, but the heart of Christianity has always been some form of martyrdom — because that is the form of Christ's love for the world. Martyrdom does not necessarily mean the need to literally die for the Faith. Rather, martyrdom can have a broader meaning for the Christian life whereby we die to self so that another may live. Martyrdom, then, becomes the particular way we let the cross of Christ take shape in us.

The cross's centrality in the Christian life is expressed from the very first moments in which we are ushered into Christ's life through baptism, in connection to which a cross is traced on our heads. In that moment, we take on Christ's yoke as an expression of our conformity with him. This conformity continues in our reception of all the sacraments, especially the Eucharist, in which we share communion with the blood of Christ outpoured. But how do we reflect on this centrality of the cross in our lives? These days we are given unique opportunities to reflect anew on the centrality of the cross in our lives:

- Could the Lord be inviting us

through this present moment to renew our commitment to him through the cross?

- Are we being given the opportunity to once again see the cross's place at the center of Christian life?
- Could Christ be asking us to see this suffering as a purification, in the fashion of Israel's own suffering?
- If we embrace the cross at this time, might we be drawn into a deeper intimacy with Jesus, and drawn into the life of hopeful suffering once again?

Embracing the cross means that we see hope in suffering. When we embrace our mission to suffer with Christ on the cross, we become beacons of hope to a broken world. Quite certainly, we share in the cross in this pandemic, especially when our sacramental life is modified and ministry is limited. It is understandable that we will have a wide range of emotions and responses to our suffering. But our hope as Christians is that the cross is effective for us, for the Church, and for the world. Therefore, we can view this time as an opportunity to unite ourselves to Christ in a powerful way and thereby help the Church continue her saving mission.

It is important to recognize that we are often suffering in this time, and with that comes a wide range of emotional responses. And it is often from such a perspective that we act. Looking back to the lesson from Israel, we see that God used the sufferings as a means to communicate his purification. In our sufferings, have we slowed down sufficiently to actually listen to God? Instead of the immediate reaction of anger or frustration and public expression of that, we should be more reflective about our responses and the suffering we are enduring. Could it be, perhaps, that Christ is asking us to see this suffering as a purification, in the fashion of Israel's own suffering? Is he asking us to see suffering as a positive quality? Is he asking us to open ourselves to a moment of profound purification? These are only possible when we stop reacting and start with the posture of receptivity that is at the heart of the life of prayer.

We can accept the cross by asking Jesus in our prayer to help us find him in the sufferings we endure. No matter the darkness we are facing, we can say to Jesus, "Help me to find you in this." In doing so, instead of running away from suffering, we make an act of hope in the suffering, and thereby participate in Christ's salvific mission for the Church and the world.

There have been many different moments of suffering in this time. For some it has been the loss of loved ones and limited access to priests, or the inability to celebrate a funeral Mass with loved ones. For others, school closures, or canceled or limited weddings and ordinations, have been the cause of real suffering. Still others have faced great pain from isolation and the inability to be with family. In particular, the elderly have found themselves cut off from care and seen as expendable.

But by embracing the cross as presented at this moment, we are often dying to self for the good of others. We do this when we do what is needed to protect others — wear masks, limit our gatherings, reduce our activities, isolate ourselves when we show signs of illness, etc. We embrace the cross for the good of others when we sacrifice our comforts for the sake of the most vulnerable, such as the elderly, those with pre-existing conditions, or those without means for medical care.

We embrace the cross for the love of God and others. "The cross is the school of love," said Saint Maximilian Kolbe, the man who laid down his life in a Nazi concentration camp so a fellow prisoner could live. As Christ taught us: "Whoever wishes to come after me must deny himself, take up his cross, and follow me" (Mt 16:24). Or consider the love Christ called us to when he said, "No one has greater love than this, to lay down one's life for one's friends" (Jn 15:13). Accepting inconvenience to our way of life can be seen as an act of love, not a violation of our freedom. True freedom is when we lay down our lives, in whatever way, for others. As Saint Clare of Assisi put it: "Love that cannot suffer is not worthy of that name."

Ensuring the lives of those who are most vulnerable is not easy. It demands that we give up even the things that give life. But that is the heart and mission of the cross. And through our sacrifice, we can be assured that the secret workings of grace abound. Grace is able to do most of its work when we are at our most helpless, when we are truly crucified, weak, and able to do nothing. Remember, on the cross Jesus was helpless and weak. Yet it was from this cross that Christ worked his greatest grace: the salvation of the world. When Christ is most helpless, there he works the greatest grace. The same is true for us. When we embrace our helplessness and simply accept it, uniting it to the cross, God is able to work great graces in the world.

By living in hope, we are united in the cross, and we hear Jesus say to us "my suf-

fering is a suffering in you." With our sufferings joined to Christ, we share in his
central mission, which is the Church's, too.
That makes suffering not just a means for
our sanctification, but also for the Church
and the world. Our embrace of the cross is
never simply for our own good. It is always
oriented toward and rooted in Christ's offering for the many. To embrace the cross,
then, is a fruit of our reception of the Eucharist over many years, drawing us more
deeply into Christ's self-offering.

Thus we must always keep the cross
at the heart of our lives, and even more so
in this moment of suffering. In the cross,
Christ does not abandon us, but is actually
and intimately united to us in a special way,
whereby we share in his mission for the salvation of the world. The cross of this time
of pandemic is difficult, but our Christian
response is not fear-mongering, nor is it a
dismissive attitude. Rather, it is the position
of hope that looks confidently for Christ in
the midst of any suffering and responds in
love. In the end, as Saint Robert Bellarmine

taught, "The school of Christ is the school of love."

SOME SPIRITUAL LESSONS

The monks and nuns of the Carthusian order, founded by Saint Bruno in 1084, live a cloistered, monastic life under the motto: *Stat crux dum volvitur orbis* ("The cross is steady while the world is turning"). In this adage we recall the centrality of the cross, not only in Christians' lives but also as the central point of all human history and all of our endeavors. In our quarantines and social distancing, amid the many problems arising from the pandemic, we can allow our spiritual lives to be revitalized by that same Carthusian wisdom.

With the cross as our aim and our guide, the spiritual lessons proposed by the present moment come into sharper focus. Through the cross, we can spiritually prosper amid hardship, suffering, and even chaos. Weeds have grown along with wheat at this time, so we have identified two spiritual threats and two spiritual fruits.

It is no secret that this time is bringing out a mix of emotions and responses in all of us. These responses can manifest deeper realities of our hearts — realities that have often been present unbeknownst to us. Perhaps another hidden gift of this time of pandemic is the opportunity it presents to each of us to become more attuned to our own hearts. Suffering always reveals the inner depths of the human heart. Even when those realities are difficult to face, if we live in Christian hope, we can confront even our negative attitudes and allow Jesus to use them to draw us closer to God.

In the Christian journey, we must also be aware of the threats to the spiritual life that can distract us from Christ and his cross. We can be drawn toward these especially at times of spiritual difficulty, such as the moment in which we find ourselves now. It is important to identify these threats in order to open ourselves up more fully to the realities of the cross and allow it to transform the world through the transformation of our lives.

Spiritual Narcissism

It can be tempting to focus solely on our own spiritual lives and neglect the needs of others, whether it be their physical health or their spiritual well-being. This temptation is spiritual narcissism. As we face our circumstances, unprecedented in our lifetimes, it is important to keep a proper perspective. The way in which we approach these times must be in accord with the priorities of the spiritual life. The Gospel mandate clearly puts a priority on others over ourselves. "Charity is superior to all the virtues," the *Catechism* states (see 1826). When we live with the love of Christ — who died not to save himself, but all of us — we come to live in the wisdom of Saint Paul's instruction that "faith, hope, love remain, these three; but the greatest of these is love" (1 Cor 13:13). So while it is good and holy to desire the sacraments, in the time of the pandemic, gathering communally can be of harm to the community. Allowing ecclesial life to carry on unchanged amid a pandemic of this kind can present problems for others in a variety of ways.

Spiritual narcissism is looking after our own spiritual needs but forgetting that the goal of our own needs is to feed our service to our neighbor. Spiritual narcissism means caring only for your own spiritual health and forgetting what is good for our brother and sister. It can manifest itself in those who think that holiness comes only from frequent reception of the sacraments, and who, as a result, demand the sacraments as a right (not a gift), no matter the cost. It forgets both the gift of baptism already at work in us, the total gift of Christ given to us when we last received the Eucharist, and God's ability to work outside of the ordinary means he has established.

This spiritual danger prioritizes the self over others, and often manifests itself in contempt of the hierarchy of the Church, especially the bishops who govern the Church as successors of the apostles. This attitude has no place in the Christian faith, which is itself apostolic. Moreover, Christ can transform us if we are open to hearing his call to conversion. Self-referential spirituality forgets the principle of charity that is at the heart of Christian living, where we look to the good of the other as our primary good and concern. This is a major spiritual issue, which we must continue to address.

When we are faced with the temptation of spiritual narcissism, what can we do? First, we can find ways to grow in humility. Naturally, we should put ourselves in the shoes of others. We should not be afraid to engage and ask questions of our leaders before we judge their decisions as wrong. We can actively look for ways to be of service and to minister to others at this difficult time, perhaps expressing our concern and love to others with a note, a call, or another act of kindness. And we should spend more time in prayer, examining our consciences, asking ourselves how God is speaking to us right now and whether or not we are living as he desires.

Acedia

Another spiritual difficulty many have encountered in the pandemic is the temptation toward the sin of acedia. Although many refer to this as sloth, acedia is the Eastern term better encompassing a deep spiritual problem many of us face: ceasing to desire the good. Acedia can refer, then, to the attitudes of sloth, laziness, apathy, or other symptoms of avoiding the good. Acedia can manifest itself in a slowness of life and an inability to do much of anything. Or it can manifest itself in great busyness, often without focus or thoroughness. Regardless, it makes us avoid the good whenever it is presented to us.

The quiet of lockdown and social distancing during the pandemic may have brought out acedia in our hearts, making us uncomfortable. Ask yourself: Has the slowness of life brought about a deepening of my spiritual life or an increase in charity? Or have I avoided the pursuit of these goods in favor of distractions? Whatever your answers, there is no need to be afraid. If we look at these things with the eyes of Christ and see his gaze of love, we can recognize the manifestation of these spiritual maladies as the first step in growing in intimacy with Jesus, who purifies us and slowly draws us into his life.

We are called to appreciate the gifts God gives, on account of their goodness, for their own sake, and in accordance with their purpose. It is truly then that we find the happiness God desires for us and can advance in the way of holiness. Part of our Christian responsibility is to assist Christ in the sanctification of all the world, even time itself, by making proper use of those gifts and dedicating them to God's purposes.

How can we overcome acedia? We can choose to pray first thing each morning, making God our first choice, which sets a proper tone for the day. Simple tasks such as limiting our use of social media and cell phones can not only remove the distractions that feed acedia but can bring peace from an often confusing, divisive, and poisonous discourse that can destroy the soul. We can choose positive things such as going for a walk, exercising, or doing something that brings wholesome joy. In doing these things, we realize the good is worth chasing after, and we train ourselves to choose it more each day. Finally, by embracing simplicity in our lives, we can better choose that which matters most and will endure. This helps remove the distractions and choices that interfere with our ability to choose God and respond to our vocation above all.

Simplicity of Life

One spiritual fruit this moment offers is the opportunity to live more simply. Many people, especially families, have frequently noted how nice it has been to have life slow down. Such slowness is important because it forces us to ask ourselves what really matters and what really is worth living for.

It also demands that we take more responsibility where our faith is concerned. This means that we must choose to pray, create a schedule of prayer, educate ourselves and our families in the Faith, reach out to fellow Catholics, etc. The choice to live the Faith is one that must be intentional with each passing day.

One way to live the simplicity of life to which God calls us is to make prayer and Catholic formation staples of our household. The liturgical calendar of the Church offers a plethora of formation opportunities. Whether it be celebrating or learning about different saints throughout the year, or using the breviary to give meaning to our day, the Church's liturgy offers an amazing way for us to enter into the rhythm of the Christian life. As extracurricular activities will be diminished for the foreseeable future, parents in particular have an opportunity to take Christian formation into their own hands as an essential duty.

In setting aside some nonessential

aspects of life, and even some that many consider essential, all of our lives have become simpler to varying degrees. This is not a bad thing in and of itself. In seizing this reality, we can make more room for God in our lives. Simpler lives can lead to greater spiritual goods, as the tradition of monastic existence has shown. In different ways, all of us have become adherents to the Benedictine maxim *ora et labora* (pray and work) as the pattern for our days. Like those who have found the fruits of monastic existence in their lives throughout the Christian centuries, we can also allow the search for God to be more present in our daily lives. We can all do well to strip away things until we can allow God to calm our restless hearts. May we come to learn the wisdom of the Psalmist who proclaims, "My soul rests in God alone" (Ps 62:2).

Leisure can help us achieve such a focus on what is most important in life — in fact, really at the heart of it. Slowing down and simplifying life frees up time for what is truly essential. Leisure does not mean binging on a streaming service, or mindlessly filling the time with endless internet scrolling. Leisure is more substantial than that. Leisure is a real rest, whereby we enter into God's rest (see Gn 2:2). It is time set aside for things that are good in and of themselves: spending time with family, simply lying about contemplating the beauty of God's creation, reading something that builds us up, renewed focus on prayer, etc. Leisure means to rest in things that are not practical, but are worthy pursuits for their own sake and lead us closer to God.

This importance of leisure is a difficult lesson for us to learn. We are formed by the idea that we are what we do, and that doing is essential to our very identity. We forget that being is greater than doing. The reemergence of the simplicity of life as a byproduct of the pandemic is an opportunity to rediscover the importance of being, too. And this can be found in leisure. Because of our "doing" mentality, just lying on the grass for an hour and looking

at the sky can feel like a waste of time —
but it isn't. There is nothing wasteful in
true leisurely activities because they train
us to be contemplative again. They help us
perceive God more deeply, and to see him
at work in and through his creation. Since
leisure trains us to be receptive to God and
to see him more clearly, it trains us for one
of the most important activities of leisure
— namely, prayer.

Centrality of Prayer

One final fruit that can arise in this time
of pandemic is greater understanding of
and reliance on the centrality of personal
prayer. The closure of parishes posed this
question to each individual: Do I want to
pray? For some, prayer during this time
has been fruitful, while for others — often
for very good reasons — it has been great-
ly challenging. Many find it difficult to
build a life of prayer at home because they
don't know how to pray on their own — in
part due to a failure of Church leadership
to form people in the basics of prayer.

As the pandemic continues and our prayer lives are challenged, regardless of how well we have been formed to pray, we must ask: Am I going to seek Jesus now that the normal avenues through which I used to find him are not available to me? Let us embrace the fact that this moment can form us and challenge us to take more seriously the role of personal prayer in our lives and in our families.

There are a variety of ways in which we can pray, as many of us have learned during the pandemic. We can pray with Scripture, using *lectio divina,* or some other method; we can pray the Liturgy of the Hours or the Rosary; or we can simply set aside quiet time to listen to Jesus. SimplyCatholic.com is a great resource for more information on any of these kinds of prayer. The quiet form of prayer may be the most foreign and difficult to us. To simply sit down and listen can be a challenge. This is why vocal forms of prayer can train us to be attentive to God's voice speaking to us. We are embodied creatures, and often we need to engage our senses as we begin to pray. But once we have begun to pray in these forms, we can begin to hear the voice of God in our hearts in the quiet time we set aside for him.

To establish a habit of prayer, it is important to attempt to set aside time every day (the same time each day, if possible) to establish a regularity and a rhythm to our efforts. Perhaps we can also set aside a special place in our homes, where we keep a Bible, prayer books, or sacred images. Our relationship with God — like any relationship — can only grow insofar as we give God regular, consistent time to speak to him and to listen to him. We have a choice to make, ultimately, and this present moment has made clear how much we must choose prayer. There are no guarantees in life, save the choices we make with God.

These spiritual lessons, in addition to many others, show how God is active even amid our problems, and how he is working something good in our own hearts and in the heart of the Church. Yes, this is a time of purification and repentance, but it is also a time whereby God is drawing us back to his heart in unexpected ways. We must keep our face firmly fixed on Jesus Christ. He is our hope, he is really and truly with us, and we can really find him in this moment, if only we are willing to see.

LESSONS FROM SAINT DAMIEN OF MOLOKAI

The lessons presented to us by the pandemic are nothing new. They show up throughout history, particularly in the lives of the saints, who put into practice, in simple and heroic ways, the lessons Christ teaches us and wants us to learn as we continue to follow him. Through reflection on and imitation of their holiness and virtue, the saints lead us to ponder the ultimate goal of our Christian life — which is, of course, heaven. Particularly relevant to our purposes, then, considering the context of his own life and ministry, is Saint Damien of Molokai.

The events of 2020 are eerily similar to those that formed the backdrop of Saint

Damien's life: the spread of a mysterious and vicious disease, quarantines, missteps and poor planning by government and ecclesiastical officials, resultant civil unrest — all on top of the regular challenges and difficulties of daily living. As we wrestle with the challenges of the unfolding pandemic, Damien offers us a model for how to respond.

Born Jozcf De Veuster near Tremelo, Belgium, the future Saint Damien grew up a gregarious boy with a zest for life. Once a skating champion, Jozef was athletic and strong, qualities that would suit him well for his future work in the Molokai leper colony. His preparations for his future life also included an introduction to the sickness and death that would occupy his days among Hawaii's lepers, as he lost two sisters to various epidemics.

Brought up in a faithful family, the future saint chose to follow in the footsteps of his older brother and entered religious life with the Congregation of the Sacred Hearts of Jesus and Mary in 1859. He took Damien as his religious name. His goal was to serve in the missions, and he was known to pray each day for the grace to be like the great missionary Saint Francis Xavier. In 1863, although not yet ordained, Damien volunteered for the Hawaiian missions, taking the place of his priest-brother who could not go due to ill health.

Damien arrived in Honolulu on Saint Joseph's Day (March 19) in 1864 and was ordained a priest at the city's cathedral that May. Though he spent most of the next decade pastoring his flock, he was restless and wanted to give more of himself to God's people. He was given the opportunity to do just that when Hawaiian Bishop Louis Maigret expressed his desire for a priest to serve victims of leprosy who had been exiled into quarantine on the island of Molokai. The bishop chose not to assign anyone to this work, but instead asked for volunteers, knowing the assignment was tantamount to a death sentence. Damien joyfully and heroically offered himself, leaving for Molokai on May 10, 1873 — the date which later became his liturgical memorial. He would thenceforth be known as the apostle to the lepers.

Leprosy posed a real threat to the residents of Hawaii. Then thought incurable, the disease came in a few different forms, the most widespread of which was an ongoing decay of the living human body. And it was spreading without doctors knowing how. The disease's victims were taken from their homes and assigned as outcasts on a remote portion of the island of Molokai. Most never again saw their families. A slow, painful, lonely death awaited them.

Arriving on Molokai, Damien entered a living hell. Though the state-run quarantine's management was the prerogative of the local government, Damien found much to be desired. Human dignity was not a priority. The government's handling of the leper colony eventually played into political strife and rebellions.

He found the lepers living hopeless lives, suffering from intense psychological anguish resulting from abandonment and bodily suffering. When he arrived at Molokai, Damien also found copious amounts of sin and violence among the exiles, including drunkenness, lewd conduct, sexual promiscuity, and abusive behavior, especially toward the weakest in their midst. Molokai was lawless because it was a place without hope. No one cared enough to change that — until Damien arrived. Things began to change in part because of his work and advocacy, but ultimately because he brought Christ with him.

As an icon of Christ among the outcasts, Damien offered hope and a reason for living. He restored dignity to those who suffered from leprosy, seeing them as men and women made in God's image. And he loved them with a father's heart.

Damien's heart was moved by love. In his fatherly concern, Damien wanted to bring an end to the deplorable living conditions he found among the residents of the Molokai quarantine. Totally shut off from the world, the castaways awaited their fate, and most saw no point in their suffering. As bodies piled up or were placed in shallow graves, the stench of death permeated the colony. Among Damien's first actions after arriving there was to dig graves and provide proper burials, showing that love for God's children extends even beyond death.

Damien was a shepherd the sheep desperately needed. The organization he brought to the community raised the standard of living that the government had failed to bring the leper colony. Slowly he planted faith, hope, and love among the local unfortunates by bringing structure to the community. He built houses and orphanages, chapels and churches. He furthered infrastructure, building a pipeline and tank for clean water. He bandaged wounds and distributed clothing. He offered a contrast to other local Church leaders who were most concerned about winning approval from the local government and had an obsession with worldly administrative issues. For Damien, charity was his work first and foremost. He knew well that, as Saint Paul says, without charity, we are nothing (see 1 Cor 13:2).

Temperamentwise, Damien could be sensitive and consoling, but he also could be sharp-tongued, and he had a temper. Damien also was pastorally keen and knew what the people needed. He was especially attuned to the spiritual complacency to which members of his flock could so easily fall prey. His long, fire-and-brimstone sermons dramatically called people to conversion.

Damien's life was not his own. He gave his all for the lepers on Molokai. Damien radically conformed himself to the power of God's love, which was manifested in his own life. His decision to minister to the lepers was an acceptance of a death sentence. He did not know what he might encounter, but he knew the likelihood was very high that he, too, would succumb to the disease. And indeed he did. Damien was well prepared for the leprosy that slowly killed him over the span of five years.

Damien's self-offering came from true interior freedom, which is, as Pope Saint John Paul II described in a 1995 homily, "not in doing what we like, but in having the right to do what we ought." This freedom arose in him from a heart ablaze with love. He would often say before his death, "How sweet to die a child of the Sacred Hearts of Jesus and Mary." That bore great fruit, as Damien modeled the qualities of those holy hearts by pouring out his life as a testimony to the worth of those in his care in the eyes of God. His example teaches us a great deal about charity and concern for our brothers and sisters, which is particularly relevant during this time of pandemic.

In willingly adopting a lifelong quarantine to serve the lepers on Molokai, Damien radically gave of himself. He left behind the community life that he loved, but he never gave up hope of restoring that community. He requested time and again to have another priest join him in his work, which was never about himself. He remarked how the loneliness he encountered, particularly when he became a leper himself, was worse than any disease. He was particularly pained by the absence of priestly ministry for himself. Often left for long periods without the availability of sacramental reconciliation, he would confess his sins at the foot of the tabernacle. He experienced a radical emptiness so that the victims of leprosy did not have to experience it. This is the same emptiness to which all followers of Christ are called as we carry the cross. Damien found joy, peace, and happiness in giving far more than he received. He wrote to his brother, "People pity me and think me unfortunate, but I think of myself as the happiest of missionaries."

Throughout the years of his ministry on Molokai, Damien's primary motivation was his relationship with Jesus Christ. Because of this, acceptance of the cross was not negotiable. His life was a constant search for Christ in the poorest of the poor. He found Christ in the rejected and destitute victims of leprosy on Molokai. Damien embodied the Beatitudes, and he was defined by the characteristics expected of us at the last judgment.

In order to do what needed to be done,

Damien needed the bedrock of a deep spiritual life, and he was grounded in a serious program of spiritual growth. As a student, he once engraved on a bench, "silence, recollection, presence of God." According to the "Pastoral Rule" that Damien made for himself, he spent more time in prayer than he did doing the works for which so many remember him. And that makes perfect sense. For without his unity with the Lord through prayer and the sacraments, and without growing in knowledge and imitation of God through study and reading of Scripture, Damien could not have survived his time on Molokai. Yet he encountered God amid so much darkness, and that is what made him a saint. Damien gives us a model to follow — to prioritize our days, even while busy with duties and responsibilities, with prayer and service. Such prioritization grounds us and gives us purpose as we are conformed more and more to Christ.

It must be noted that Damien's own determination to offer his life for his flock does not represent a perfect parallel to the situation for priests in our present pandemic. Many priests put themselves in danger to administer the sacraments to the faithful, even in the early stages of the pandemic. But there was also a need for clergy to be extraordinarily cautious in ministry — not out of concern for themselves, but out of concern that they might be spreading the virus unknowingly to their flocks. Especially in the earliest days, there was little scientific evidence about the means of infection. Still, some modern-day Damiens suit up with protective gear and commit themselves exclusively to ministry among COVID-19 patients, some even doing so around the clock. Other priests are unable to do so, mostly because of age and personal preexisting health conditions, or they might be the only priest in a given area.

For nearly sixteen years, Damien challenged the leprosy victims in his corner of the Lord's vineyard to be better. His primary role was to lead the lepers closer to Christ, whom they encountered through him. Their suffering was transformed into having purpose, and this led them along the path of hope in eternal life. By the time Damien died, the majority of Molokai was Catholic.

Death came for Damien on April 15, 1889. He was forty-nine, already an internationally acclaimed humanitarian. Though he was originally buried under the indigenous pandandus tree where he slept during his first nights on Molokai, his remains were moved to his homeland in 1936 at the request of the Belgian king. Saint Damien of Molokai was canonized in 2009 by Pope Benedict XVI.

Damien passed up many opportunities to leave Molokai, ever zealous to win souls for Christ. But his sacrifice was an embodiment of the sacrifice of Christ, who tells us, "No one has greater love than this, to lay down one's life for one's friends" (Jn 15:13). Of this, Pope Saint John Paul II remarked at Damien's 1995 beatification: "What could he have offered the other lepers, who were condemned to a slow death, if not his own faith and this truth that Christ is Lord and that God is love? He became a leper among the lepers; he became a leper for the lepers. He suffered and died like them, believing that he would rise again in Christ, for Christ is the Lord!"

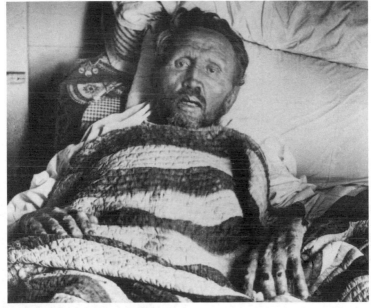

Conclusion

We hope that these brief reflections have offered an opportunity to pause and find Christ in the crisis brought on by the COVID-19 pandemic. As people of faith, our task always is to see where God is active and to trust that he provides for our every need. While hindsight provides 20/20 vision, we can also take stock in the midst of situations such as this pandemic by learning from the experience of God's people throughout salvation history. And moments like this allow us to recognize the gifts Christ gives us. We are challenged anew to discover the spiritual tools that Christ bestows on the members of his body.

Such gifts at our disposal in the Christian life are both foundational to what we believe and also often taken for granted — especially in the midst of difficulties forced upon us by situations such as the current pandemic.

As disciples we are called to follow Christ's way more and more each day, and that is, of course, ultimately the way of the cross. That Christian journey is the way of charity, service, and sacrifice. We are strengthened and spurred on by the concrete examples of fellow travelers on this way, those holy men and women who have carried Christ's cross for the good of their brothers and sisters. As we face the days ahead, with their uncertainty and continued opportunities for suffering and spiritual growth, may our decisions and perspectives align with the primacy of charity articulated by Saint Paul. That is, in the end, the love of Christ and his cross, the love that has motivated and sustained the saints — the very love in which we are daily called to persevere.

Spiritual Resources

PRAYER DURING A PANDEMIC

Lord Jesus,

Hear our pleas, our good shepherd and divine physician. We implore your mercy in the wake of an outbreak of serious illness and disease.

Guide our efforts to prevent contagion and make preparations to care for those most vulnerable. Assist all professionals and volunteers who work to eradicate the epidemic now spreading. May our actions be marked by your steadfast love and selfless service and never by panic or fear.

Bestow your comfort and healing upon the sick; sustain and strengthen them by your grace. May they know your closeness as they carry the cross of illness.

And may all you have called from this life come to worship you eternally with all the saints as you grant consolation and peace to their mourners. Amen.

A PLAGUE LITANY

By Father James Goodwin
(Originally published on SimplyCatholic. com)

Lord, have mercy. *Lord, have mercy.*
Christ, have mercy. *Christ, have mercy.*
Lord, have mercy. *Lord, have mercy.*
Christ, hear us. *Christ, hear us.*
Christ, graciously hear us. *Christ, graciously hear us.*
God the Father in heaven, *have mercy on us.*
God the Son, Redeemer of the world, *have mercy on us.*
God the Holy Spirit, *have mercy on us.*
Holy Trinity, one God, *have mercy on us.*

Holy Mary, Mother of God, *pray for us.*

Holy Mary, Help of the Sick, *pray for us.*

Holy Mary, Health of the Roman People, *pray for us.*

Holy Mary, Our Lady of Perpetual Help, *pray for us.*

Holy Mary, Consoler of the Afflicted, *pray for us.*

Saint Joseph, Spouse of the Virgin Mary, *pray for us.*

Saint Joseph, Hope of the Sick, *pray for us.*

Saint Joseph, Patron of the Dying, *pray for us.*

Saint Joseph, Terror of Demons, *pray for us.*

Saint Michael, light and hope of souls near death, *pray for us.*

Saint Michael, our most sure aid, *pray for us.*

Saint Michael, receiver of the souls of the elect after death, *pray for us.*

Saint Raphael, God's remedy, *pray for us.*

Saint Gabriel, God's messenger, *pray for us.*

Guardian Angel, my protector, *pray for us.*

All you holy angels, *pray for us.*

Saint George, valiant martyr of Christ, *pray*

for us.

Saint Blaise, zealous bishop and benefactor of the poor, *pray for us.*

Saint Erasmus, mighty protector of the oppressed, *pray for us.*

Saint Pantaleon, miraculous exemplar of charity, *pray for us.*

Saint Vitus, special protector of chastity, *pray for us.*

Saint Christopher, mighty intercessor in dangers, *pray for us.*

Saint Dionysius, shining mirror of faith and confidence, *pray for us.*

Saint Cyriacus, terror of hell, *pray for us.*

Saint Acacius, helpful advocate in death, *pray for us.*

Saint Eustace, exemplar of patience in adversity, *pray for us.*

Saint Giles, despiser of the world, *pray for us.*

Saint Margaret of Antioch, valiant champion of the Faith, *pray for us.*

Saint Catherine of Alexandria, victorious defender of the Faith and of purity, *pray for us.*

Saint Barbara, mighty patroness of the dying, *pray for us.*

All you Fourteen Holy Helpers, *pray for us.*

Saint Luke, patron of physicians, *pray for us.*

Saint Agatha, patroness of nurses, *pray for us.*

Saint Martin De Porres, patron of public health, *pray for us.*

Saint Roch, who did expose your life to heal the sick, *pray for us.*

Saint Sebastian, comforter of the dying, *pray for us.*

Saint Corona, patroness of plague victims, *pray for us.*

Saint Benedict, protector of those who cry to you, *pray for us.*

Saint Charles Borromeo, whose selflessness during a great plague won the hearts even of your foes, *pray for us.*

Saint Gregory the Great, whose prayers ended a plague, *pray for us.*

Saint Aloysius Gonzaga, who died as a result of caring for the sick, *pray for us.*

Saint Rosalie, by whose intercession a plague was ended, *pray for us.*

Saint Casimir, known for generosity to the sick, *pray for us.*

Saints Cosmas and Damian, holy brother-physicians, *pray for us.*

Saint Camillus de Lellis, patron of the sick and health care workers, *pray for us.*

Saint John of God, patron of hospitals, *pray for us.*

Saint Frances of Rome, dedicated to the sick and the poor, *pray for us.*

Saint Quirinus of Neuss, patron of those affected by plague, *pray for us.*

Saint Anthony the Great, patron of those infected by disease, *pray for us.*

Saint Edwin the Martyr, patron of pandemics, *pray for us.*

Saint Damien of Molokai, compassionate to the sick and outcasts, *pray for us.*

Saint Godeberta of Noyon, who miraculously brought an end to a plague, *pray for us.*

Saint Henry Morse, who cared for plague victims, *pray for us.*

Saint Marianne Cope, who saw in the sick the face of Jesus, *pray for us.*

Blessed Francis Xavier Seelos, holy priest
who died caring for the sick, *pray for us.*
Blessed Engelmar Unzeitig, chaplain amid
an outbreak at Dachau, *pray for us.*
All holy saints of God, *pray for us.*
From every evil, *Lord, save your people.*
From every sin, *Lord, save your people.*
From your anger, *Lord, save your people.*
From sudden and unforeseen death, *Lord,
save your people.*
From the snares of the devil, *Lord, save your
people.*
From anger, hatred, and all ill will, *Lord,
save your people.*
From the spirit of uncleanness, *Lord, save
your people.*
From lightening and tempest, *Lord, save
your people.*
From the scourge of earthquake, *Lord, save
your people.*
From plague, famine, and war, *Lord, save
your people.*
From everlasting death, *Lord, save your
people.*
Be merciful to us sinners, *Lord, hear our*

prayer.

That you will spare us, *Lord, hear our prayer.*

That you will pardon us, *Lord, hear our prayer.*

That it may please you to bring us to true repentance, *Lord, hear our prayer.*

To deliver our souls from eternal damnation, and the souls of our brethren, kinsmen, and benefactors, *Lord, hear our prayer.*

To give and preserve the fruits of the earth, *Lord, hear our prayer.*

To grant eternal rest to all the faithful departed, *Lord, hear our prayer.*

Lamb of God, who takes away the sins of the world: *spare us, O Lord.*

Lamb of God, who takes away the sins of the world: *graciously hear us, O Lord.*

Lamb of God, who takes away the sins of the world: *have mercy on us.*

Let us pray.

Almighty and eternal God, our refuge in every danger, to whom we turn in our distress, in faith, we pray, look with compassion on the afflicted, grant eternal rest to the dead, comfort to mourners, healing to the sick, peace to the dying, strength to health care workers, wisdom to our leaders, and the courage to reach out to all in love, so that together we may give glory to your Holy Name. Through our Lord Jesus Christ, your Son, who lives and reigns with you in the unity of the Holy Spirit, one God, for ever and ever.

SCRIPTURE FOR REFLECTION DURING A PANDEMIC

Further Reference on the Babylonian Exile

Daniel 1:1–7

Jeremiah 29:4–14

Various Passages from 1 & 2 Chronicles

Building Up Christian Hope

Romans 8:18–30

Romans 8:35–39

2 Corinthians 4:16–18

2 Corinthians 12:7–10

1 Peter 1:3–6

Christian Unity of Heart

1 Corinthians 1:10–12

Philippians 2:1–5

About the Authors

Father Harrison Ayre is a priest of the Diocese of Victoria (Canada) where he is currently a pastor and cohost of the *Clerically Speaking* podcast. He has two degrees in theology from Newman Theological College. He is a frequent contributor to OSV's Simply Catholic and is a Ph.D. student at Maryvale Institute, studying Joseph Ratzinger's theology of the human person.

Michael R. Heinlein is editor of OSV's Simply Catholic and has a degree in theology from The Catholic University of America. Experienced in parish ministry and high school education, Michael is a frequent contributor to OSV publications and recently authored *The Handy Little Guide to Spiritual Communion*. Most important to him is his role as husband and father.